LIFE
GIVING
RELATIONSHIPS

WITH CONTRIBUTORS FROM

ASSOCIATION OF RELATED CHURCHES

CONTENTS

FOREWORD

In 2000, I had a crazy vision. I thought God wanted my church—Seacoast Church in Charleston, South Carolina—to plant 2,000 churches. I had no idea how to go about making that vision happen, but God did. Today, over 400 churches strong, ARC is an association of relational churches working with church planters and church leaders to provide support, guidance, and resources.

With more than 110 million Americans never or rarely attending church, it's critical that we cross cultural walls to reach the lost. ARC is all about helping churches stay culturally relevant—characterized by Bible-based teaching, authentic relationships, and dynamic family ministries.

We recognize that solid relationships are the foundation for growth in any aspect of life. So we decided to capture what God is teaching us about relationships—with family, friends, nonbelievers, and others.

Throughout this series, you'll hear insights from both ARC leaders and our ministry friends. We represent an ever-expanding group of people who are committed to one another's success. Join us as we discover what lifegiving relationships are all about.

GREG SURRATT
President,
Association of Related Churches (ARC)

ARC LEAD TEAM

 Greg Surratt
Seacoast Church

 Peter Haas
Substance Church

 Randy Bezet
Bayside Community
Church

 Chris Hodges
Church of the
Highlands

 Rick Bezet
New Life Church

 Scott Hornsby
Fellowship Church
Zachary

 **Nick &
Christine Caine**
A21 Campaign

 Matt Keller
Next Level Church

 Joe Champion
Celebration Church

 Rob Ketterling
River Valley Church

 Herbert Cooper
People's Church

 John Siebeling
The Life Church

 Matt Fry
C3 Church

 Stovall Weems
Celebration Church

LIFEGIVING **RELATIONSHIPS**

5

SPECIAL THANKS TO SESSION CONTRIBUTORS: John and Lisa Bevere, Brady Boyd, Lori Champion, Tiffany Cooper, Wilfredo & Elizabeth De Jesús, Martha Fry, Willie George, Steve Harval, Steve Kelly, Becca Ketterling, Dave Martin, Todd Mullins, Leslie Siebeling, Ken Vance, Philip & Holly Wagner.

INTRODUCTION

WELCOME TO LIFEGIVING RELATIONSHIPS!

When I look back at the months it has taken to put together this study series, I'm grateful to be surrounded with such a great team of people who have spoken into these sessions. Not only individuals, but couples have been authentic in front of a camera and given us a glimpse into the realities of how God works in the middle of and through the complications of lifegiving relationships. These individuals have shared their lives and their passion, and I can hardly wait to see how God is going to use all this to bring more people into the Kingdom!

All of life in all its amazing forms owes its existence to God. He not only gives life, but He gives it meaning and purpose. There are no random or accidental instances of life. God is behind them all and wants to heighten and deepen our experience of life. Jesus said in John 10:10, "I have come that they may have life, and have it to the full." This series will allow you a fresh look at just how true His words are. Father, Son, and Holy Spirit are fully engaged in offering to us life "to the full" and gifts that are lifegiving.

This isn't about life-getting or receiving. You will be called to give, to participate. Remember Jesus' words, "Give, and it will be given to you. A good measure, pressed down, shaken together and running over, will be poured into your lap. For with the measure you use, it will be measured to you" (Luke 6:38). Take this opportunity to meet with other Christians and provoke each other to love and good deeds. Ask God to help you not miss what He has planned for you in your lifegiving relationships.

MARC CLEARY
Director of Development,
Association of Related Churches (ARC)

HOW TO USE THIS
STUADY GUIDE

THIS STUDY GUIDE'S CONTENTS ARE DIVIDED INTO SECTIONS:

SESSIONS:
The sessions are designed to complement the DVD teaching and be easy to follow. Use this book as a guide, not a straitjacket. If the group responds to the lesson in an unexpected but honest way, go with that. If you think of a better question than the one shown, ask it.

EXTRA HELPS:
Familiarize yourself with the various items included in this section. You may wish to incorporate some of them into the sessions themselves. Take to heart the insights included in the small group leader helps and the Frequently Asked Questions page.

If you are facilitating/leading a small group, this section will give you advice from experienced leaders both to encourage you and help you avoid many common obstacles to effective small group leadership.

OUTLINE OF
EACH SESSION

A TYPICAL GROUP SESSION FOR LIFEGIVING RELATIONSHIPS
WILL INCLUDE THE FOLLOWING:

THEME VERSE AND INTRODUCTION. For each session we have
provided an overview and a theme verse that emphasizes one of
our lifegiving relationships. Memorizing Scripture can be a vital part
of filling our minds with God's will for our lives.

GROWING TOGETHER WITH DVD TEACHING SEGMENT. This
section features the Lifegiving Relationships DVD teaching
segments from the ARC lead team and other contributors. They'll
share insights and experiences to help you better understand and
consider how God wants us to be lifegiving in our relationships.
Questions will guide you as a group to process the teaching you
heard and saw.

LEARNING TOGETHER. Here you'll focus on a passage of Scripture
(or two) related to the topic. You'll look at what the Bible says
about the topic, asking and answering questions to deepen your
understanding.

SHARING TOGETHER. How do you live out what you've learned?
This section will guide you to apply the truths you are learning.
You'll apply the insights from Scripture practically, creatively, and
from your heart as well as your head.

FOR PERSONAL REFLECTION. This section will allow you to
process prayerfully what you've learned on your own. You may
want to use a journal to record your thoughts as you consider how
God is leading you to apply this truth to your life.

DAILY DEVOTIONS. Each week on the Daily Devotions pages
we provide Scriptures to read and reflect on between group
meetings. We suggest you use this section to seek God on your
own throughout the week. This time at home should begin and end
with prayer. Don't get in a hurry; take enough time to hear God's
direction.

LIFEGIVING
FRIENDSHIPS

"GREATER LOVE HAS NO ONE THAN THIS: TO LAY DOWN ONE'S LIFE FOR ONE'S FRIENDS." JOHN 15:13

When Jesus was asked which was the most important of all the Mosaic laws, He said that there were two that were inseparable: Love God with all you've got, and love others as yourself. You couldn't do one and not the other. If you said you loved God but didn't love others, you were simply fooling yourself.

Loving others brings us great joy, but it's also just plain difficult because all of us are imperfect, flawed human beings. It is in this context of community that we learn to become more like Jesus. Think about the fruit of the Spirit discussed in Galatians 5: Love, joy, peace, patience. Many are only evident in relationships. It's not that hard to be patient if you're alone—it's when you have to be patient with someone (and that person is being difficult) that you see whether there is actually any real evidence of patience in your life. It is there—where we are learning to be patient, or loving, or kind—that we experience God, and we grow. Living out the fruit of the Spirit is just one way we become a lifegiving friend.

When you were growing up, who was your best friend? What drew you together? What kept you connected?

What qualities do you look for in a good friend?

GROWING
TOGETHER

God wants us to experience friendships centered on Him that bring us joy and life. These lifegiving friendships provide more than companionship or company. They can provide healing to our souls. While most of us would say we want relationships like that, we are sometimes hesitant to take steps toward those friendships. They require us to risk and to be vulnerable, which we can only do with God's help.

In each session, we'll hear from church leaders who share what they have discovered about lifegiving relationships as they follow Jesus.

WATCH THE DVD FOR THIS SESSION

CAPTURE THOUGHTS YOU WANT TO REMEMBER ABOUT LIFEGIVING FRIENDSHIPS.

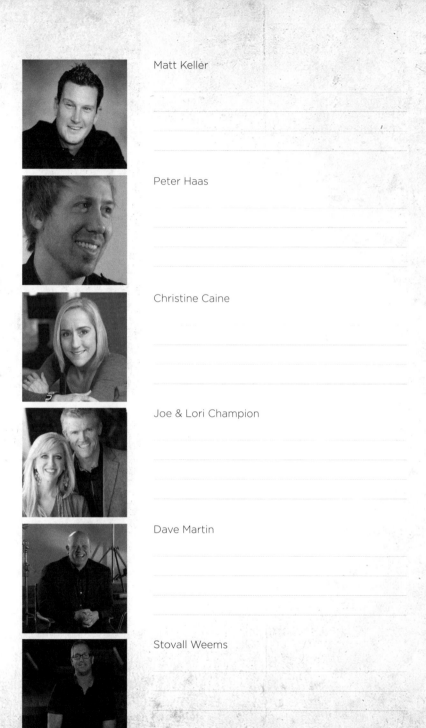

Matt Keller

Peter Haas

Christine Caine

Joe & Lori Champion

Dave Martin

Stovall Weems

What characteristics of lifegiving
friendships did these individuals identify?

Joe and Lori Champion challenged us
to "show yourself friendly" in order to
find friends. How can we show ourselves
friendly to others?

Peter Haas shared that he was convicted
by James 5:16: "Therefore confess your
sins to each other and pray for each
other so that you may be healed. The
prayer of a righteous person is powerful
and effective." Peter opened up to his
friends. How can accountability like this be
lifegiving?

What keeps us from living out this verse in
friendships?

LEARNING
TOGETHER

LIFEGIVING FRIENDSHIP COMES WHEN WE EXPERIENCE WHAT GOD'S WORD TEACHES.

READ COLOSSIANS 3:12–15

[12] Therefore, as God's chosen people, holy and dearly loved, clothe yourselves with compassion, kindness, humility, gentleness and patience. [13] Bear with each other and forgive one another if any of you has a grievance against someone. Forgive as the Lord forgave you. [14] And over all these virtues put on love, which binds them all together in perfect unity. [15] Let the peace of Christ rule in your hearts, since as members of one body you were called to peace. And be thankful.

According to this passage, what is our identity? Who are we, and what have we received?

What do you think it means to "bear with each other"? How might having a friend who bears with you and forgives you make that friendship more lifegiving?

READ EPHESIANS 4:29–32
29 Do not let any unwholesome talk come out of your mouths, but only what is helpful for building others up according to their needs, that it may benefit those who listen. 30 And do not grieve the Holy Spirit of God, with whom you were sealed for the day of redemption. 31 Get rid of all bitterness, rage and anger, brawling and slander, along with every form of malice. 32 Be kind and compassionate to one another, forgiving each other, just as in Christ God forgave you.

Which positive characteristics of friends does this passage identify? How about negative characteristics?

How can "unwholesome talk" or gossip drain life from our relationships?

How does the Holy Spirit help us to be a "life giver" in our friendships?

SHARING
TOGETHER

Based on everything we've discussed, what do lifegiving friendships look like?

What is one thing you need to change (with the Holy Spirit's help) that would make you a more lifegiving friend to others?

How can the group pray for you? (Add the prayer requests here.)

CLOSE IN PRAYER.

FOR PERSONAL
REFLECTION

What effects are you personally hoping to see as a result of your participation in this small group experience?

Think about your three closest current friendships. Rate each on a scale of 1 to 10, with 1 being "life-draining" and 10 being "extremely lifegiving."

Now use the same scale and predict how your friends would score your friendship with them. Would they rate your friendship the same? Why or why not?

TO BECOME A MORE LIFEGIVING FRIEND, WHICH OF THE FOLLOWING NEXT STEPS WILL YOU TAKE?

«   I will write a list of characteristics I'd like to develop in myself to be a lifegiving friend to others.

«   I will prayerfully and honestly evaluate my current friendships to determine which are lifegiving and which are not.

«   I will write a list of characteristics I'd like to develop in myself to be a lifegiving friend to others.

«   I will reach out to a friend I already have to initiate "going deeper" in our friendship.

«   Other: _____

DAILY
DEVOTIONS

Developing our ability to serve God through the leading of the Holy Spirit takes time and persistence. The lifegiving part comes to us day-by-day as we:

Pray. Commit to personal prayer and daily connection with God. (You may find it helpful to write your prayers in a journal.) Remember to pray for the requests shared by your fellow group members.

Memorize. Reflect on what God is saying about lifegiving friendships by learning a passage of Scripture.

"Greater love has no one than this: to lay down one's life for one's friends." John 15:13

Daily Devotions. Complete the Daily Devotions section. Each day, you'll read just one portion of a passage of Scripture. Give prayerful consideration to what God is telling you. Take your time! Ponder and reflect. Then record your thoughts, insights, or prayer in the Reflect section below the verses you read. On the sixth day, record a summary of what you have learned about lifegiving friendships through this study.

DAILY
DEVOTIONS

Day 1.

1 JOHN 3:11
"For this is the message you heard from the beginning: We should love one another."

REFLECT:
It sounds simple to just "love one another," but this is a challenging assignment at times. Sometimes our own past experiences hinder us. What makes it hard for you to love others?

Day 2.

1 JOHN 3:12–13
"Do not be like Cain, who belonged to the evil one and murdered his brother. And why did he murder him? Because his own actions were evil and his brother's were righteous. Do not be surprised, my brothers and sisters, if the world hates you."

REFLECT:
How does comparison drain life from relationships? Have you ever felt jealous of someone else's righteousness? What's one step you can take to let go of comparing yourself to others?

Day 3.

1 JOHN 3:14
"We know that we have passed from death to life, because we love each other. Anyone who does not love remains in death."

REFLECT:
You can be alive physically, but "remain in death." Have you ever felt spiritually dead? How can loving others revive us spiritually?

Day 4.

1 JOHN 3:15
"Anyone who hates a brother or sister is a murderer, and you know that no murderer has eternal life residing in him."

REFLECT:
This verse might remind us of Jesus' teaching in the Sermon on the Mount: "I tell you that anyone who is angry with a brother or sister will be subject to judgment." (see Matthew 5:21-24). How do words of hatred "kill" or drain life from others? Of the people in your life, who might you be draining life from with your words or actions? How can those relationships become more lifegiving?

Day 5.

1 JOHN 3:16
"This is how we know what love is: Jesus Christ laid down his life for us. And we ought to lay down our lives for our brothers and sisters."

REFLECT:
While we may not be called to actual martyrdom, what does it mean to lay down your life for someone? Why is it hard to lay down our agenda or our need to be right for our friends?

Day 6.

SUMMARY:
Use the following space to write any thoughts God has put in your heart and mind about lifegiving friendships.

TAKING ACTION:
What is one thing you will do as a result of what you've heard from God?

SESSION 2
LIFEGIVING
MARRIAGE

THAT IS WHY A MAN LEAVES HIS FATHER AND MOTHER AND IS
UNITED TO HIS WIFE, AND THEY BECOME ONE FLESH. ADAM
AND HIS WIFE WERE BOTH NAKED, AND THEY FELT NO SHAME.
GENESIS 2:24-25

Marriage was God's idea all the way back to the beginning. The
world may be busy trying to sell marriage as meaningless or magic,
but those who pay attention to the Bible know that marriage is
both life demanding and lifegiving when pursued in God's way.

When we come to a discussion of marriage within the boundaries
of lifegiving faith, we often have to set aside many of the
assumptions or misunderstandings the world presents as models
for marriage. For example, romance and feelings are significant
components in marriage, but they are not the life in a marriage.
Lifegiving marriage involves at its heart a continual and growing
commitment to God and to one another that remains in place even
in the ebb and flow of romance and feelings. God gave us marriage
as a primary relationship in which we can live out our relationship
with Him.

Almost everyone has an "unforgettable couple" story. What
marriage(s) have left the biggest impact on you and why?

If you had to describe your spouse's strengths in three words,
what words would you choose?

GROWING
TOGETHER

Living in a culture where the divorce rate for Christians and non-Christians alike is about 50 percent, just staying married is a challenge.

But God wants more for our marriages than just gutting it out, living under the same roof. He doesn't just want us to stay together, He wants us to grow together. He wants our marriages to be lifegiving—a source of joy and energy and fulfillment.

God designed marriage not only to fulfill our desire for intimacy, but to provide a picture of His intimacy with His people. God's ideal for marriage is oneness—a wonderful interdependence where we each give to the other.

We can't have a marriage like that on our own—we need God's help. The good news is, He's eager to give us everything we need to be able to love our spouses well.

WATCH THE DVD FOR THIS SESSION

CAPTURE THOUGHTS YOU WANT TO REMEMBER ABOUT LIFEGIVING MARRIAGE.

Rob & Becca Ketterling

Wilfredo (Choco) & Elizabeth De Jesús

John & Lisa Bevere

Phillip & Holly Wagner

Herbert & Tiffany Cooper

What practical tips for a lifegiving
marriage did these individuals identify?

One term used frequently by these
couples was "communication." What have
you discovered about communication in
marriage?

Several individuals highlighted the need
to handle conflict in healthy ways. Why is
conflict an unavoidable aspect of marriage
and therefore something we must learn
how to manage?

Awareness and honesty are additional keys
to a lifegiving marriage. What happens
when these are lost in the shuffle of
modern life?

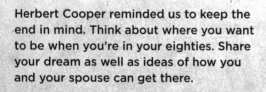

Herbert Cooper reminded us to keep the
end in mind. Think about where you want
to be when you're in your eighties. Share
your dream as well as ideas of how you
and your spouse can get there.

LEARNING
TOGETHER

THE FOUNDATION FOR A LIFEGIVING MARRIAGE COMES FROM GOD'S WORD.

READ MATTHEW 19:3–6

[3] Some Pharisees came to him to test him. They asked, "Is it lawful for a man to divorce his wife for any and every reason?"

[4] "Haven't you read," he replied, "that at the beginning the Creator 'made them male and female,' [5] and said, 'For this reason a man will leave his father and mother and be united to his wife, and the two will become one flesh'? [6] So they are no longer two, but one flesh. Therefore what God has joined together, let no one separate."

What do each of these three phrases mean in marriage?

- "leave his father and mother"
- "united to his wife"
- "and the two will become one flesh"

How might the meanings differ in describing a couple on their wedding day compared to their fiftieth wedding anniversary?

What is the appropriate role of parents in a lifegiving marriage?

READ COLOSSIANS 3:18-21

18 Wives, submit yourselves to your husbands, as is fitting in the Lord. 19 Husbands, love your wives and do not be harsh with them. 20 Children, obey your parents in everything, for this pleases the Lord. 21 Fathers, do not embitter your children, or they will become discouraged.

What general principles about relationships does this passage give us?

Based on verses 18 and 19, what would you say is harder to do: submit as a wife or love as a husband?

A parallel passage in Ephesians 5 tells husbands to love their wives as Christ loved the church. How would you describe Christ's love for the church? What would it mean to love your spouse in this way?

What does Paul have in mind when he tells dads not to "embitter your children"?

As one couple said in the video, it's important to remember that being head of a household doesn't mean a husband is more important or valuable or even above his wife.

SHARING
TOGETHER

Based on all we've discussed, what are characteristics of a lifegiving marriage relationship?

What is one step you need to take (with the Holy Spirit's help) to be a more loving—or lifegiving—spouse?

Since we're thinking about lifegiving marriages, what are two or three crucial things we should all be praying for our marriages?

How can the group pray for you? (Add the prayer requests here.)

CLOSE IN PRAYER.

FOR PERSONAL
REFLECTION

It's easy to blame the other person when a relationship is difficult. Knowing that God loves you and wants the best for you, spend some time asking Him to show you one or two things that you need to change about your behavior in your marriage.

WHAT ADDITIONAL STEPS WILL YOU TAKE TO HAVE A MORE LIFEGIVING MARRIAGE?

« I will prayerfully and honestly evaluate my marriage to determine whether my attitudes and actions are lifegiving.

« I will write a list of characteristics I'd like to develop in myself to be a more lifegiving spouse.

« I will ask my spouse to tell me what I can do to make our marriage more lifegiving.

« Other: _____

DAILY
DEVOTIONS

Developing a lifegiving marriage comes to us day-by-day as we:

Pray. Commit to praying for your marriage each day. Also remember to pray for the requests shared by your fellow group members. (You may find it helpful to write your prayers in a journal.)

Memorize. Reflect on what God is saying about lifegiving marriage by learning a passage of Scripture.

That is why a man leaves his father and mother and is united to his wife, and they become one flesh. Adam and his wife were both naked, and they felt no shame. Genesis 2:24–25

Daily Devotions. Complete the Daily Devotions section. Each day, give prayerful consideration to what God is telling you. Ponder and reflect. Then record your thoughts, insights, or prayer in the Reflect section below the verses you read. On the sixth day, record a summary of what you have learned about lifegiving marriage through this study.

DAILY
DEVOTIONS

Day 1.

PROVERBS 18:22

"He who finds a wife finds what is good and receives favor from the LORD."

REFLECT:

In what ways have you received favor from the Lord through your spouse?

Day 2.

1 PETER 3:7

"Husbands, in the same way be considerate as you live with your wives, and treat them with respect as the weaker partner and as heirs with you of the gracious gift of life, so that nothing will hinder your prayers."

REFLECT:

In what ways are you sharing the "gracious gift of life" with your spouse?

Day 3.

GENESIS 2:24–25

"That is why a man leaves his father and mother and is united to his wife, and they become one flesh. Adam and his wife were both naked, and they felt no shame."

REFLECT:

How do you see the "leaving," "uniting," and "becoming one" parts of a lifegiving marriage?

Day 4.

HEBREWS 13:4
"Marriage should be honored by all, and the marriage bed kept pure, for God will judge the adulterer and all the sexually immoral."

REFLECT:
Why do you think the Bible insists marriage should be honored by all?

Day 5.

EPHESIANS 5:32–33
"This is a profound mystery—but I am talking about Christ and the church. However, each one of you also must love his wife as he loves himself, and the wife must respect her husband."

REFLECT:
In what ways do you think a loving husband and a respectful wife bring life to a marriage?

Day 6.

SUMMARY:
Use the following space to write any thoughts God has put in your heart and mind about lifegiving marriage.

TAKING ACTION:
What is one thing you will do as a result of what you've heard from God?

LIFEGIVING
FAITH

AND WITHOUT FAITH IT IS IMPOSSIBLE TO PLEASE GOD, BECAUSE ANYONE WHO COMES TO HIM MUST BELIEVE THAT HE EXISTS AND THAT HE REWARDS THOSE WHO EARNESTLY SEEK HIM. HEBREWS 11:6

People may think that faith means turning away from reality, as if faith were a deliberate denial of life. But when we try to reduce our experiences in this world to simple naturalistic explanations like chemical processes and random instincts, life quickly loses meaning.

When Jesus told us He came that we might have life and have it more abundantly, He was talking about the life of faith—faith in Him. The kind of trusting awareness that reaches beyond our senses into spiritual reality makes all the difference in the way we live on earth. Faith connects us with the power of the Holy Spirit and enables us to do far more than we ever thought possible. It is the foundation of our most important lifegiving relationship—our relationship with God.

When did you first become aware of God and His love for you? What was your first step of faith—a step toward relationship with Him?

What barriers get in the way of faith? What makes it hard to trust and believe God?

GROWING
TOGETHER

God calls us to live a life of faith. The Bible says He seeks to "strengthen those whose hearts are fully committed to him" (2 Chronicles 16:9) He not only wants us to have faith, but He wants to support and strengthen us.

Lifegiving faith grows by testing. When we step out in faith, God shows Himself faithful, and we grow in our ability to trust. Our faith can't grow by just talking about it. We need to do more than just hear about God's Word—we need to do what it says. That's what really makes our faith lifegiving.

In the video, we'll hear from church leaders who share what they have discovered about lifegiving faith.

WATCH THE DVD FOR THIS SESSION

CAPTURE THOUGHTS YOU WANT TO REMEMBER ABOUT LIFEGIVING FAITH.

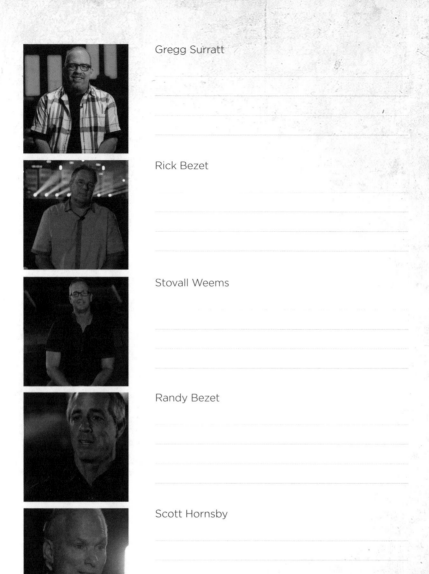

Gregg Surratt

Rick Bezet

Stovall Weems

Randy Bezet

Scott Hornsby

Greg Surratt references Hebrews 11:1, a
common definition of faith. How would you
define faith?

Stovall Weems used the history of the
church in Ephesus to talk about the idea
of "first love," a phrase Jesus used in
Revelation 2:4. What is the connection
between our "first love" and lifegiving
faith?

Both Randy Bezet and Scott Hornsby
challenge us to believe for great things
from God. How might this require our faith
to be lifegiving?

LEARNING
TOGETHER

READ EPHESIANS 2:1–10

[1] As for you, you were dead in your transgressions and sins, [2] in which you used to live when you followed the ways of this world and of the ruler of the kingdom of the air, the spirit who is now at work in those who are disobedient. [3] All of us also lived among them at one time, gratifying the cravings of our flesh and following its desires and thoughts. Like the rest, we were by nature deserving of wrath. [4] But because of his great love for us, God, who is rich in mercy, [5] made us alive with Christ even when we were dead in transgressions—it is by grace you have been saved. [6] And God raised us up with Christ and seated us with him in the heavenly realms in Christ Jesus, [7] in order that in the coming ages he might show the incomparable riches of his grace, expressed in his kindness to us in Christ Jesus. [8] For it is by grace you have been saved, through faith—and this is not from yourselves, it is the gift of God— [9] not by works, so that no one can boast. [10] For we are God's handiwork, created in Christ Jesus to do good works, which God prepared in advance for us to do.

Verses 1–3 describe a person apart from Christ as dead. What could we say about the faith of someone whose life looks more like the one Paul described here?

How do we access lifegiving faith, according to verses 4 and 5? What are the differences between trying to be saved *through* good works and realizing one has been saved *for* good works? What are some of the "good works" God has prepared in advance for you to do?

READ JAMES 2:14–17

[14] What good is it, my brothers and sisters, if someone claims to have faith but has no deeds?Can such faith save them? [15] Suppose a brother or a sister is without clothes and daily food. [16] If one of you says to them, "Go in peace; keep warm and well fed," but does nothing about their physical needs, what good is it? [17] In the same way, faith by itself, if it is not accompanied by action, is dead.

What is the difference between faith as some kind of intellectual exercise and faith as lifegiving?

If something stops growing, it dies. What specific actions will keep your faith alive and growing?

How does meeting the physical needs of people demonstrate our faith? How would our loving actions help their faith to grow as well?

SHARING
TOGETHER

Looking at the six specific themes we will visit in this series (friendships, marriage, faith, generosity, ministry, and mission), which do you least connect with your current understanding of faith? Why?

What step of faith (and perhaps risk) is God prompting you to take in order to experience a deeper lifegiving faith?

How does worshipping God strengthen our faith? How will you worship God, both corporately and privately, in the next week?

How can the group pray for you? (Add the prayer requests here.)

CLOSE IN PRAYER.

FOR PERSONAL
REFLECTION

Think about a season in your life when you felt your faith was at a "peak." What caused that?

WHICH OF THE FOLLOWING NEXT STEPS WILL YOU TAKE WHEN IT COMES TO LIFEGIVING FAITH?

«   I will prayerfully and honestly evaluate my relationship with God and consider my levels of trust, obedience, and joy.

«   I will write a list of characteristics I'd like to develop in myself (with God's help) to grow in my lifegiving faith.

«   I will take one "faith step" in the coming week, to take actions that require me to trust God.

«   Other: _____

DAILY
DEVOTIONS

Developing our ability to serve God through the leading of the Holy Spirit takes time and persistence in getting to know our Lord. The lifegiving part comes to us day-by-day as we:

Pray. Commit to personal prayer and daily connection with God. (You may find it helpful to write your prayers in a journal.) Remember to pray for the requests shared by your fellow group members.

Memorize. Reflect on what God is saying about lifegiving faith by learning a passage of Scripture.

And without faith it is impossible to please God, because anyone who comes to him must believe that he exists and that he rewards those who earnestly seek him. Hebrews 11:6

Daily Devotions. Complete the Daily Devotions section. Each day, give prayerful consideration to what God is telling you. Ponder and reflect. Then record your thoughts, insights, or prayer in the Reflect section below the verses you read. On the sixth day, record a summary of what you have learned about lifegiving faith through this study.

DAILY
DEVOTIONS

Day 1.

EPHESIANS 2:8–9
"For it is by grace you have been saved, through faith—and this is not from yourselves, it is the gift of God—not by works, so that no one can boast."

REFLECT:
How would you describe the greatest gift of all?

Day 2.

JOHN 10:10
"The thief comes only to steal and kill and destroy; I have come that they may have life, and have it to the full."

REFLECT:
How have you experienced the effects of the "thief's" work in your life? What three words come to mind in describing the life you have in Christ?

Day 3.

COLOSSIANS 2:6–7
"So then, just as you received Christ Jesus as Lord, continue to live your lives in him, rooted and built up in him, strengthened in the faith as you were taught, and overflowing with thankfulness."

REFLECT:
When you look back on your own experience of salvation, what if anything is missing now in the way of daily dependence on God? How does this verse picture lifegiving faith?

For more Lifegiving Relationships videos, go to lifegivingrelationships.net/devotions

Day 4.

DEUTERONOMY 30:19–20

"This day I call the heavens and the earth as witnesses against you that I have set before you life and death, blessings and curses. Now choose life, so that you and your children may live and that you may love the LORD your God, listen to his voice, and hold fast to him. For the LORD is your life, and he will give you many years in the land he swore to give to your fathers, Abraham, Isaac and Jacob."

REFLECT:
When Moses said, "choose life," what was he talking about in the context of lifegiving faith?

Day 5.

JOHN 14:6

"Jesus answered, 'I am the way and the truth and the life. No one comes to the Father except through me.'"

REFLECT:
Why is it crucial to remember that lifegiving faith must be rooted in Jesus and no one else?

Day 6.

SUMMARY:
Use the following space to write any thoughts God has put in your heart and mind about lifegiving faith.

TAKING ACTION:
What is one thing you will do as a result of what you've heard from God?

LIFEGIVING
GENEROSITY

A GENEROUS PERSON WILL PROSPER; WHOEVER REFRESHES OTHERS WILL BE REFRESHED. PROVERBS 11:25

For many people, the subject of generosity is like quicksand. They think if they dip a toe into generosity, they will drown. But the Bible makes generosity one of the marks of spiritual maturity. We may say we believe in a God who can meet all our needs, but most of us never put ourselves in a situation where we actually need that to be true!

Lifegiving generosity is not an obligation, but an opportunity. When we practice generosity, we won't feel deprived. We'll feel excited to be partnering with God to further His kingdom. Let's not miss the adventure of giving generously.

If you had $10,000 to give away, who would you give it to and why?

Tell about a time someone was generous to you. How did you feel? How did you respond?

GROWING
TOGETHER

We serve a generous God. Think of the precious gift of life that Jesus gave you by dying on the cross. Think of the blessings God's given you, His abundant love.

When we've been recipients of such generosity, shouldn't our response be to turn and be generous to others? To give back to God and His work?

Lifegiving generosity requires a "not mine" mind-set. When we see ourselves as stewards, rather than owners, we realize that even our ability to earn money, buy things, and accumulate wealth are themselves blessings from God.

In the video, you'll hear from ministry leaders who have learned the benefits of lifegiving generosity.

WATCH THE DVD FOR THIS SESSION

CAPTURE THOUGHTS YOU WANT TO REMEMBER ABOUT LIFEGIVING GENEROSITY.

Rick Bezet

Ken Vance

Randy Bezet

Peter Haas

Willie George

Based on the teaching for this session,
what would you say are keys to
maintaining an attitude of generosity?

How did you respond to Peter Haas's
story about God leading his wife and him
to give away their nest egg as an act of
obedience?

Willie George shared that generosity is
about more than giving money. How is
it easiest for you to be generous? Which
ways are the most difficult?

Discuss together how an individual
follower of Jesus might discern between
giving what is possible, giving until it
hurts, or giving until it's gone.

LEARNING
TOGETHER

JESUS TAUGHT MORE ABOUT MONEY THAN ALMOST ANY
OTHER TOPIC. WE CAN GROW IN LIFEGIVING GENEROSITY BY
EXPERIENCING HIS TEACHING AND LIVING IT OUT.

READ MATTHEW 6:19-24

[19] "Do not store up for yourselves treasures on earth, where moths
and vermin destroy, and where thieves break in and steal. [20] But
store up for yourselves treasures in heaven, where moths and
vermin do not destroy, and where thieves do not break in and steal.
[21] For where your treasure is, there your heart will be also.

[22] "The eye is the lamp of the body. If your eyes are healthy, your
whole body will be full of light. [23] But if your eyes are unhealthy,
your whole body will be full of darkness. If then the light within you
is darkness, how great is that darkness!

[24] "No one can serve two masters. Either you will hate the one and
love the other, or you will be devoted to the one and despise the
other. You cannot serve both God and money."

In verse 19, what does Jesus point out as glaring problems with setting our hearts on earthly treasures?

How would you go about "storing up treasures in heaven"?

How would you characterize a person whose heart is in heaven?

Jesus said you cannot serve both God and money. What do you think it means to "serve money"?

READ 1 JOHN 3:16-18

[16] This is how we know what love is: Jesus Christ laid down his life for us. And we ought to lay down our lives for our brothers and sisters. [17] If anyone has material possessions and sees a brother or sister in need but has no pity on them, how can the love of God be in that person? [18] Dear children, let us not love with words or speech but with actions and in truth.

What does this passage tell us should motivate our acts of giving?

We often think of "pity" as simply feeling sorry for someone. But what does John mean when he writes about having pity on someone in need?

What does it mean to love with actions and in truth?

SHARING
TOGETHER

If someone outside the group asked you to describe what the term "lifegiving generosity" means, what would you say?

Even if people don't know the level of our generosity, what should motivate our willingness to meet the needs we see?

How can we develop a more generous spirit?

How can we become more generous with our material possessions? Our time? In relationship with others?

How can the group pray for you? (Add the prayer requests here.)

CLOSE IN PRAYER.

FOR PERSONAL
REFLECTION

On a scale of 1 to 5, with 1 meaning you never give anything, and 5 meaning you give more than 10 percent of your income away, how generous are you with your money? How about with your time? Your things?

We often become fearful when we think about giving generously. What scares you most about giving?

DAILY
DEVOTIONS

Developing lifegiving generosity begins and grows as we:

Pray. Commit to praying about being more generous. Remember to pray for the requests shared by your fellow group members. (You may find it helpful to write your prayers in a journal.)

Memorize. Reflect on what God is saying about lifegiving generosity by learning a passage of Scripture.

A generous person will prosper; whoever refreshes others will be refreshed. Proverbs 11:25

Daily Devotions. Complete the Daily Devotions section. Each day, read the daily verses and give prayerful consideration to what God is telling you. Ponder and reflect. Then record your thoughts, insights, or prayer in the Reflect section below the verses you read. On the sixth day, record a summary of what you have learned about lifegiving generosity through this study.

DAILY
DEVOTIONS

Day 1.

MATTHEW 10:8

"Heal the sick, raise the dead, cleanse those who have leprosy, drive out demons. Freely you have received; freely give."

REFLECT:

How does your own practice of generosity reflect all that has been done for you, not only by God but by others who have "freely given" to you?

Day 2.

HEBREWS 12:1–2

"Therefore, since we are surrounded by such a great cloud of witnesses, let us throw off everything that hinders and the sin that so easily entangles. And let us run with perseverance the race marked out for us, fixing our eyes on Jesus, the pioneer and perfecter of faith. For the joy set before him he endured the cross, scorning its shame, and sat down at the right hand of the throne of God."

REFLECT:

How is lifegiving generosity like running a distance race?

Day 3.

PROVERBS 6:1–5

"My son, if you have put up security for your neighbor, if you have shaken hands in pledge for a stranger, you have been trapped by what you said, ensnared by the words of your mouth. So do this, my son, to free yourself, since you have fallen into your neighbor's hands: Go—to the point of exhaustion—and give your neighbor no rest! Allow no sleep to your eyes, no slumber to your eyelids. Free yourself, like a gazelle from the hand of the hunter, like a bird from the snare of the fowler."

REFLECT:

In what ways do these proverbs point to entanglements that make generosity impossible?

For more Lifegiving Relationships videos, go to
lifegivingrelationships.net/devotions

Day 4.

2 CORINTHIANS 9:7–9
"Each of you should give what you have decided in your heart to give, not reluctantly or under compulsion, for God loves a cheerful giver. And God is able to bless you abundantly, so that in all things at all times, having all that you need, you will abound in every good work. As it is written: 'They have freely scattered their gifts to the poor; their righteousness endures forever.'"

REFLECT:
In what ways would you say your giving is cheerful?

Day 5.

PROVERBS 11:25
"A generous person will prosper; whoever refreshes others will be refreshed."

REFLECT:
How has your generosity led to both prosperity and refreshment from the Lord in your life?

Day 6.

SUMMARY:
Use the following space to write any thoughts God has put in your heart and mind about lifegiving generosity.

TAKING ACTION:
What is one thing you will do as a result of what you've heard from God?

LIFEGIVING
MINISTRY

AND LET US CONSIDER HOW WE MAY SPUR ONE ANOTHER ON TOWARD LOVE AND GOOD DEEDS, NOT GIVING UP MEETING TOGETHER, AS SOME ARE IN THE HABIT OF DOING, BUT ENCOURAGING ONE ANOTHER—AND ALL THE MORE AS YOU SEE THE DAY APPROACHING. HEBREWS 10:24-25

We don't have to be a vocational minister in order to have a ministry. When we serve those in need, share our faith with the lost, encourage the weary—we are engaging in ministry.

These deeds can be the source of great fulfillment, but also great challenge. If we approach ministry with wrong motives, or do more than God calls us to in an effort to impress Him (or others), we may find that ministry experiences become life robbing rather than lifegiving.

But when we take time to unpack the experiences and examine the expectations, the calling, and the context of ministry experiences, we usually find that the problem isn't ministry. The problem is in our expectations, our approach, and our limitations.

Are we willing to listen to what God calls us to do (and not run ahead to do things He never asked us to do)? Then we'll discover the joy of lifegiving ministry.

How has someone ministered to you in a lifegiving way?

Share about a time you served in a ministry that was exciting and vibrant, in which you saw great results—in other words, a lifegiving ministry.

GROWING
TOGETHER

We are getting to the risky, direction-changing part of taking action that involves ministry. Loving is the ultimate proactive strategy in the world. And we usually don't have to go very far to begin practicing what God has expected us to do all along—love.

God has filled the Bible with examples, teaching, commands, and instructions regarding the kind of love He expects us to exercise and the settings where it should be present. Our challenge is to take Him at His Word, follow His example, and practice love as He has instructed.

A big part of lifegiving ministry happens when we serve the body of Christ. It is not just a part or component of life—it is life itself. When we make ministry our lifestyle, we begin to understand our God-given purposes on this earth.

WATCH THE DVD FOR THIS SESSION

CAPTURE THOUGHTS YOU WANT TO REMEMBER ABOUT LIFEGIVING MINISTRY HERE.

LIFEGIVING **RELATIONSHIPS**

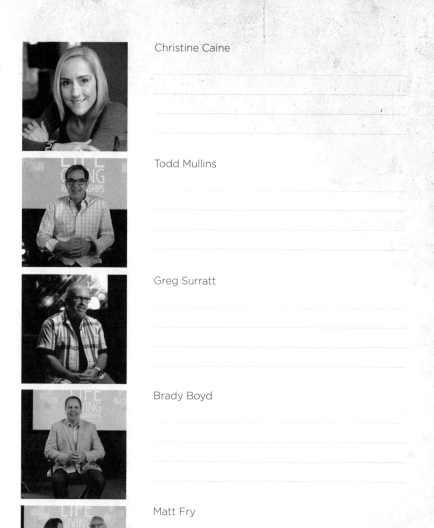

Christine Caine

Todd Mullins

Greg Surratt

Brady Boyd

Matt Fry

What characteristics of lifegiving ministry
were identified in the video? Do you agree
or disagree with their conclusions?

What practical suggestion are you most
likely to put into practice yourself?

Why do you think some people approach
church as consumers, expecting a high
payoff with little direct involvement or
investment themselves?

Greg Surratt shared how he discovered
his ministry was life-draining rather than
lifegiving. What are signs of life-draining
ministry? How can we avoid this dryness?

LEARNING
TOGETHER

TAKE SOME TIME TO DIG INTO THE TRUTH OF GOD'S WORD TOGETHER, LOOKING TO JESUS' EXAMPLE OF WHAT IT MEANS TO MINISTER TO OTHERS.

READ JOHN 13:1–17

[1] It was just before the Passover Festival. Jesus knew that the hour had come for him to leave this world and go to the Father. Having loved his own who were in the world, he loved them to the end.

[2] The evening meal was in progress, and the devil had already prompted Judas, the son of Simon Iscariot, to betray Jesus. [3] Jesus knew that the Father had put all things under his power, and that he had come from God and was returning to God; [4] so he got up from the meal, took off his outer clothing, and wrapped a towel around his waist. [5] After that, he poured water into a basin and began to wash his disciples' feet, drying them with the towel that was wrapped around him.

[6] He came to Simon Peter, who said to him, "Lord, are you going to wash my feet?"

[7] Jesus replied, "You do not realize now what I am doing, but later you will understand."

[8] "No," said Peter, "you shall never wash my feet." Jesus answered, "Unless I wash you, you have no part with me."

[9] "Then, Lord," Simon Peter replied, "not just my feet but my hands and my head as well!"

[10] Jesus answered, "Those who have had a bath need only to wash their feet; their whole body is clean. And you are clean, though not every one of you." [11] For he knew who was going to betray him, and that was why he said not every one was clean.

[12] When he had finished washing their feet, he put on his clothes and returned to his place. "Do you understand what I have done for you?" he asked them. [13] "You call me 'Teacher' and 'Lord,' and rightly so, for that is what I am. [14] Now that I, your Lord and Teacher, have washed your feet, you also should wash one another's feet. [15] I have set you an example that you should do as I have done for you. [16] Very truly I tell you, no servant is greater than his master, nor is a messenger greater than the one who sent him. [17] Now that you know these things, you will be blessed if you do them."

What did Jesus say with His actions in these verses? What was the main point of His words?

What did Jesus mean when He said that we should wash one another's feet? What did this foot washing symbolize?

How did Jesus connect the reality of our relationships with Him with the realities of our relationships with one another?

READ ROMANS 12:1
¹ Therefore I urge you, brothers and sisters, in view of God's mercy, to offer your bodies as a living sacrifice, holy and pleasing to God.

How does this verse emphasize the sacrificial side of serving others?

How can we practice being a living sacrifice without burning out?

SHARING
TOGETHER

Name some talents God has given people that can be used when serving others. Where are the various places of service where those talents would be useful?

Is genuine lifegiving ministry doing what people recruit you to do or is it finding places where you can do what God designed you to do?

Our theme verse for this session talks about "spurring" and encouraging one another in ministry. What is one way that you could spur someone else to good deeds? How might your service in ministry do that?

How can the group pray for you? (Add the prayer requests here.)

CLOSE IN PRAYER.

FOR PERSONAL
REFLECTION

Lifegiving ministry connects the needs of others with our talents and passions. What talents do you have that could help meet the needs of others?

In some seasons, we serve in a ministry of a church by volunteering our time. In other seasons, our ministry may be at home, to small children or an aging parent. Others minister in their workplace by praying, evangelizing, or even just loving their coworkers. Where are you ministering right now?

If you had unlimited time and resources and could do any kind of ministry, what would you want to do?

DAILY
DEVOTIONS

Our service in the ministry God has gifted us for grows as we:

Pray. Commit to praying about being involved in ministry. Remember to pray for the requests shared by your fellow group members. (You may find it helpful to write your prayers in a journal.)

Memorize. Reflect on what God is saying about lifegiving ministry by learning a passage of Scripture.

And let us consider how we may spur one another on toward love and good deeds, not giving up meeting together, as some are in the habit of doing, but encouraging one another—and all the more as you see the Day approaching. Hebrews 10:24-25

Daily Devotions. Complete the Daily Devotions section. Each day, read the daily verses and give prayerful consideration to what God is telling you. Ponder and reflect Then record your thoughts, insights, or prayer in the Reflect section below the verses you read. On the sixth day, record a summary of what you have learned about lifegiving ministry through this study.

DAILY
DEVOTIONS

Day 1.

MATTHEW 20:28
"The Son of Man did not come to be served, but to serve, and to give his life as a ransom for many."

REFLECT:
How do Jesus' words set the bar of service high for those who claim to follow Him?

Day 2.

MARK 12:29–31
"The most important one," answered Jesus, "is this: 'Hear, O Israel: The Lord our God, the Lord is one. Love the Lord your God with all your heart and with all your soul and with all your mind and with all your strength.' The second is this: 'Love your neighbor as yourself.' There is no commandment greater than these."

REFLECT:
How would someone know by examining your life that this two-part commandment is the central drive in your life?

Day 3.

COLOSSIANS 3:23–24
"Whatever you do, work at it with all your heart, as working for the Lord, not for human masters, since you know that you will receive an inheritance from the Lord as a reward. It is the Lord Christ you are serving."

REFLECT:
Between you and the Lord, how readily do you serve with all your heart?

For more Lifegiving Relationships videos, go to
lifegivingrelationships.net/devotions

Day 4.

HEBREWS 10:24–25
"And let us consider
how we may spur one
another on toward
love and good deeds,
not giving up meeting
together, as some are
in the habit of doing,
but encouraging one
another—and all the
more as you see the Day
approaching."

REFLECT:
Where in your life today
do you need to take a
more intentional step in
ministry toward others?

Day 5.

JOHN 13:34–35
"A new command I
give you: Love one
another. As I have loved
you, so you must love
one another. By this
everyone will know that
you are my disciples, if
you love one another."

REFLECT:
What opportunities
are you finding to love
others? How is love-
giving the highest form
of lifegiving?

Day 6.

SUMMARY:
Use the following space
to write any thoughts
God has put in your
heart and mind about
lifegiving ministry.

TAKING ACTION:
What is one thing you
will do as a result of
what you've heard from
God?

All-Access Conference attendees praying for Pastor Rick Warren.

LIFEGIVING
MISSION

"THEREFORE GO AND MAKE DISCIPLES OF ALL NATIONS, BAP-
TIZING THEM IN THE NAME OF THE FATHER AND OF THE SON
AND OF THE HOLY SPIRIT, AND TEACHING THEM TO OBEY EV-
ERYTHING I HAVE COMMANDED YOU. AND SURELY I AM WITH
YOU ALWAYS, TO THE VERY END OF THE AGE."
MATTHEW 28:19–20

When you experience something amazing, don't you want to
share it with others? If we find a great restaurant or vacation spot,
isn't it our instinct to recommend it to others?

If we share such mundane things as where to get a great meal,
shouldn't we be even more eager to share an experience that
changed our lives forever? If knowing Jesus has really turned our
lives around, shouldn't we want to let others know so that they
can experience the same thing?

At the heart of it, isn't that what evangelism, or mission, really is:
inviting others to experience the same life-changing encounter
that we have experienced?

Tell us about an unforgettable, unexpected spiritual conversation
you had with someone. Describe the setting and situation. How
did the conversation start, and how did it end?

GROWING
TOGETHER

Jesus calls us to be disciples who make disciples—who go wherever God calls us, to tell others about Jesus. It's an exciting mission. In this final session, we're going to talk about how engaging in that mission can be one of the most lifegiving things we'll ever experience.

WATCH THE DVD FOR THIS SESSION

CAPTURE THOUGHTS YOU WANT TO REMEMBER ABOUT LIFEGIVING MISSION HERE.

Joe & Lori Champion

John & Leslie Siebeling

Steve Harval

Steve Kelly

Matt & Martha Fry

What stood out to you about lifegiving mission?

When it comes to mission, why is mentality and attitude more important than location?

Steve Kelly talks about how vision helps us focus in our life. What is your vision for reaching others?

What was your take-away from John and Leslie Siebeling sharing about their church's outreach to hungry kids?

LEARNING
TOGETHER

READ ACTS 26:1–32

As it is read to the group, ask someone to time how long it took Paul to tell his story. The account of Paul's appearance before King Agrippa gives us a great example of how to give an account of God's work in our life. We may never get the chance to speak to a president or influential leader, but we can trust God to give us a chance to tell our story for His glory to many people along the way. If He opens the door, are we willing to tell our story?

¹ Then Agrippa said to Paul, "You have permission to speak for yourself."

So Paul motioned with his hand and began his defense: ² "King Agrippa, I consider myself fortunate to stand before you today as I make my defense against all the accusations of the Jews, ³ and especially so because you are well acquainted with all the Jewish customs and controversies. Therefore, I beg you to listen to me patiently.

⁴ "The Jewish people all know the way I have lived ever since I was a child, from the beginning of my life in my own country, and also in Jerusalem. ⁵ They have known me for a long time and can testify,

if they are willing, that I conformed to the strictest sect of our religion, living as a Pharisee. ⁶ And now it is because of my hope in what God has promised our ancestors that I am on trial today. ⁷ This is the promise our twelve tribes are hoping to see fulfilled as they earnestly serve God day and night. King Agrippa, it is because of this hope that these Jews are accusing me. ⁸ Why should any of you consider it incredible that God raises the dead?

⁹ "I too was convinced that I ought to do all that was possible to oppose the name of Jesus of Nazareth. ¹⁰ And that is just what I did in Jerusalem. On the authority of the chief priests I put many of the Lord's people in prison, and when they were put to death, I cast my vote against them. ¹¹ Many a time I went from one synagogue to another to have them punished, and I tried to force them to blaspheme. I was so obsessed with persecuting them that I even hunted them down in foreign cities.

¹² "On one of these journeys I was going to Damascus with the authority and commission of the chief priests. ¹³ About noon, King Agrippa, as I was on the road, I saw a light from heaven, brighter than the sun, blazing around me and my companions. ¹⁴ We all fell to the ground, and I heard a voice saying to me in Aramaic, 'Saul, Saul, why do you persecute me? It is hard for you to kick against the goads.'

¹⁵ "Then I asked, 'Who are you, Lord?'
" 'I am Jesus, whom you are persecuting,' the Lord replied. ¹⁶ 'Now get up and stand on your feet. I have appeared to you to appoint

you as a servant and as a witness of what you have seen and will see of me. ¹⁷ I will rescue you from your own people and from the Gentiles. I am sending you to them ¹⁸ to open their eyes and turn them from darkness to light, and from the power of Satan to God, so that they may receive forgiveness of sins and a place among those who are sanctified by faith in me.'

¹⁹ "So then, King Agrippa, I was not disobedient to the vision from heaven. ²⁰ First to those in Damascus, then to those in Jerusalem and in all Judea, and then to the Gentiles, I preached that they should repent and turn to God and demonstrate their repentance by their deeds. ²¹ That is why some Jews seized me in the temple courts and tried to kill me. ²² But God has helped me to this very day; so I stand here and testify to small and great alike. I am saying nothing beyond what the prophets and Moses said would happen— ²³ that the Messiah would suffer and, as the first to rise from the dead, would bring the message of light to his own people and to the Gentiles."

²⁴ At this point Festus interrupted Paul's defense. "You are out of your mind, Paul!" he shouted. "Your great learning is driving you insane."

²⁵ "I am not insane, most excellent Festus," Paul replied. "What I am saying is true and reasonable. ²⁶ The king is familiar with these things, and I can speak freely to him. I am convinced that none of this has escaped his notice, because it was not done in a corner. ²⁷ King Agrippa, do you believe the prophets? I know you do."

²⁸ Then Agrippa said to Paul, "Do you think that in such a short time you can persuade me to be a Christian?"

²⁹ Paul replied, "Short time or long—I pray to God that not only you but all who are listening to me today may become what I am, except for these chains."

[30] The king rose, and with him the governor and Bernice and those sitting with them. [31] After they left the room, they began saying to one another, "This man is not doing anything that deserves death or imprisonment."

[32] Agrippa said to Festus, "This man could have been set free if he had not appealed to Caesar."

How much of Paul's story was BC (before Christ) and how much AC (after Christ)?

In what ways did both Festus and Agrippa demonstrate possible responses to our testimonies?

As you think about Paul's setting and his story, what other conclusions do you draw that affect your view of God's prompting in your life?

SHARING
TOGETHER

The subject of "comfort zone" is a significant one in developing a mission outlook. How would you describe the differences between your comfort zone and your discomfort zone?

Even though Jesus gave the Great Commission (Matthew 28:19–20) to make disciples to all His followers, many of us don't have a talent for evangelism. What have you found are the most effective bridges anyone can build into another person's life that may become a passageway for the gospel?

Depending on the size of your group, do this together or divide into groups of three. Take turns giving an under-two-minutes summary of your testimony. Both the facts of our stories and the reality of telling them can affect us in many ways.

Take a few minutes to discuss the future of your group. How many of you are willing to stay together as a group and work through another study together? If you have time, turn to the Small Group Agreement on page 94 and talk about any changes you would like to make as you move forward as a group.

How can the group pray for you? (Add the prayer requests here.)

CLOSE IN PRAYER.

FOR PERSONAL
REFLECTION

What is one step you will take within the next week to move
forward in personal evangelism?

Who introduced you to Jesus? Have you ever thanked them?

Consider writing a letter or e-mail this week letting them know of
their impact on your life.

DAILY
DEVOTIONS

Day 1.

PROVERBS 19:23

"The fear of the LORD leads to life; then one rests content, untouched by trouble."

REFLECT:

Why is it important to balance our sense of purpose and mission with a continual awareness of God's place in our life?

Day 2.

ROMANS 5:8

"But God demonstrates his own love for us in this: While we were still sinners, Christ died for us."

REFLECT:

Why might this be a crucial verse to include in your story somewhere? How is mission the task of passing on God's love?

Day 3.

1 PETER 3:15

"But in your hearts revere Christ as Lord. Always be prepared to give an answer to everyone who asks you to give the reason for the hope that you have. But do this with gentleness and respect."

REFLECT:

What different phrases could you use to answer the question, "Why are you so hopeful?"

For more Lifegiving Relationships videos, go to
lifegivingrelationships.net/devotions

Day 4.

ACTS 16:31

"They replied, 'Believe in the Lord Jesus, and you will be saved—you and your household.'"

REFLECT:

Based on your story, what would you say to someone if that person wanted what you have in Christ? What does your answer say about your readiness for mission?

Day 5.

2 PETER 1:3

"His divine power has given us everything we need for a godly life through our knowledge of him who called us by his own glory and goodness."

REFLECT:

What evidence of mission mindedness has been part of your life today?

Day 6.

SUMMARY:

Use the following space to write any thoughts God has put in your heart and mind about lifegiving mission.

TAKING ACTION:

What is one thing you will do as a result of what you've heard from God?

EXTRA HELPS

LEADERSHIP
TRAINING 101

CONGRATULATIONS! YOU HAVE RESPONDED TO THE CALL TO HELP SHEPHERD JESUS' FLOCK. THERE ARE FEW OTHER TASKS IN THE FAMILY OF GOD THAT SURPASS THE CONTRIBUTION YOU WILL MAKE. AS YOU PREPARE TO LEAD, WHETHER IT IS ONE SESSION OR THE ENTIRE SERIES, HERE ARE A FEW THOUGHTS TO KEEP IN MIND. WE ENCOURAGE YOU TO READ THESE AND REVIEW THEM WITH EACH NEW DISCUSSION LEADER BEFORE THAT PERSON LEADS.

1 Remember that you are not alone. God knows everything about you, and He knew that you would be asked to lead your group. Remember that it is common for all good leaders to feel that they are not ready to lead. Moses, Solomon, Jeremiah, and Timothy—they all were reluctant to lead. God promises, "Never will I leave you; never will I forsake you" (Hebrews 13:5). Whether you are leading for one evening, for several weeks, or for a lifetime, you will be blessed as you serve.

2 Don't try to do it alone. Pray right now for God to help you build a healthy leadership team. If you can enlist a coleader to help you lead the group, you will find your experience to be much richer. This is your chance to involve as many people as you can in building a healthy group. All you have to do is call and ask people to help. You'll be surprised at the response.

3 Just be yourself. If you won't be you, who will? God wants to use your unique gifts and temperament. Don't try to do things exactly like another leader; do them in a way that fits you! Just admit it when you don't have an answer, and apologize when you make a mistake. Your group will love you for it, and you'll sleep better at night!

4   Prepare for your meeting ahead of time. Review the DVD session and the leader's notes in this guide, and write down your responses to each question. Pay special attention to exercises that ask group members to do something other than engage in discussion.

These exercises will help your group live what the Bible teaches, not just talk about it. Be sure you understand how an exercise works, and bring any necessary supplies (such as paper and pens) to your meeting. Finally review "Outline for Each Session" (page 8) so you'll remember the purpose of each section in the study.

5   Pray for your group members by name. Before you begin your session, go around the room in your mind and pray for each member by name. You may want to review the prayer list at least once a week. Ask God to use your time together to touch the heart of every person uniquely. Expect God to lead you to whomever He wants you to encourage or challenge in a special way. If you listen, God will surely lead!

6   When you ask a question, be patient. Someone will eventually respond. Sometimes people need a moment or two of silence to think about the question, and if silence doesn't bother you, it won't bother anyone else. After someone responds, affirm the response with a simple "thanks" or "good job." Then ask, "How about somebody else?" or "Would someone who hasn't shared like to add anything?" Be sensitive to new people or reluctant members who aren't ready to talk or pray in a group setting. If you give them a safe setting, they will blossom over time.

7   Provide transitions between questions. When guiding the discussion, always read aloud the transitional paragraphs and the questions. Ask the group if anyone would like to read the paragraph or Bible passage. Don't call on anyone, but ask for a volunteer, and then be patient until someone begins. Be sure to thank the person who reads aloud.

8   Break up into smaller groups each week, or people won't stay. If your group has more than seven people, we strongly encourage you to have the group gather sometimes in discussion circles of three or four people during the Sharing Together sections of the study. With a greater opportunity to talk in a small circle, people will connect more with the study, apply more quickly what they're learning, and ultimately get more out of it. A small circle also encourages a quiet person to participate and tends to minimize the effects of a more vocal or dominant member. It can also help people feel more loved in your group. When you gather again at the end of the section, you can have one person summarize the highlights from each circle.

Small circles are also helpful during prayer time. People who are unaccustomed to praying aloud will feel more comfortable trying it with just two or three others. Also, prayer requests won't take as much time, so circles will have more time to actually pray. When you gather back with the whole group, you can have one person from each circle briefly update everyone on the prayer requests. People are more willing to pray in small circles if they know that the whole group will hear all the prayer requests.

LEADING FOR
THE FIRST TIME

Sweaty palms are a healthy sign. The Bible says God is gracious to the humble. Remember who is in control; if you feel inadequate, that is probably a good sign. Those who are soft in heart (and sweaty palmed) are those whom God is sure to speak through.

Seek support. Ask your leader, coleader, or close friend to pray for you and prepare with you before the session. Walking through the study will help you anticipate potentially difficult questions and discussion topics.

Bring your uniqueness to the study. Lean into who you are and how God wants you to lead the study uniquely.

Prepare. Prepare. Prepare. Go through the session several times. If you are using the DVD, listen to the teaching segment and then choose the questions you want to be sure to discuss.

Ask for feedback so you can grow. Perhaps in an e-mail or on cards handed out at the study, have everyone write down three things you did well and one thing you could improve on. Don't get defensive, but show an openness to learn and grow.

Prayerfully consider launching a new group. This doesn't need to happen overnight, but God's heart is for this to happen over time. Not all Christians are called to be leaders or teachers, but we are all called to be "shepherds" of a few someday.

Share with your group what God is doing in your heart. God is searching for those whose hearts are fully His. Share your trials and victories. We promise that people will relate.

HOSTING
AN OPEN HOUSE

If you're starting a new group, try planning an open house before your first formal group meeting. Even if you have only two to four core members, it's a great way to break the ice and to consider prayerfully who else might be open to join you over the next few weeks. You can also use this kickoff meeting to hand out study guides, spend some time getting to know each other, discuss each person's expectations for the group, and briefly pray for each other.

A simple meal or good desserts always make a kickoff meeting more fun. After people introduce themselves and share how they ended up being at the meeting (you can play a game to see who has the wildest story!), have everyone respond to a few icebreaker questions: "What is your favorite family vacation?" or "What is one thing you love about your church/our community?" or "What are three things about your life growing up that most people here don't know?"

Next, ask everyone to tell what he or she hopes to get out of the study. You might want to review the Small Group Agreement (page 94) and talk about each person's expectations and priorities.

Finally, set an empty chair (maybe two) in the center of your group and explain that it represents someone who would enjoy or benefit from this group but who isn't here yet. Ask people to pray about whom they could invite to join the group over the next few weeks. Hand out postcards and have everyone write an invitation or two. Don't worry about ending up with too many people; you can always have one discussion circle in the living room and another in the dining room after you watch the session. Each group could then report prayer requests and progress at the end of the session.

You can skip this kickoff meeting if your time is limited, but you'll experience a huge benefit if you take the time to connect with each other in this way.

SMALL GROUP
FAQS

What do we do on the first night of our group?
Like all fun things in life—have a party! A "get to know you" coffee, dinner, or dessert night is a great way to launch a new study. You may want to review the Small Group Agreement (page 94) and share the names of a few friends you can invite to join you. But most importantly, have fun before your study time begins.

Where do we find new members for our group?
We encourage you to pray with your group and then brainstorm a list of people from work, church, your neighborhood, your children's school, family, the gym, and so forth. Then have each group member invite several of the people on his or her list.

No matter how you find participants, it's vital that you stay on the lookout for new people to join your group. All groups tend to go through healthy attrition—the result of moves, releasing new leaders, ministry opportunities, and so forth—and if the group gets too small, it could be at risk of shutting down. If you and your group stay open, you'll be amazed at the people God sends your way. The next person just might become a friend for life. You never know!

How long will this group meet?
It's totally up to the group once you come to the end of this six-week study. Most groups meet weekly for at least their first six weeks, but every other week can work as well.

At the end of this study, each group member may decide if he or she wants to continue on for another six-week study. Some groups launch relationships for years to come, and others are stepping-stones into another group experience. Either way, enjoy the journey.

What if this group is not working for us?
You're not alone! This could be the result of a personality conflict, life stage difference, geographical distance, level of spiritual

maturity, or any number of things. Relax. Pray for God's direction, and at the end of this six-week study, decide whether to continue with this group or find another. You don't buy the first car you look at or marry the first person you date, and the same goes with a group. Don't bail out before the six weeks are up—God might have something to teach you. Also, don't run from conflict or prejudge people before you have given them a chance. God is still working in you too!

How do we handle the child care needs in our group?

We suggest that you empower the group to openly brainstorm solutions. You may try one option that works for a while and then adjust over time. Our favorite approach is for adults to meet in the living room or dining room and to share the cost of a babysitter (or two) who can be with the kids in a different part of the house. In this way, parents don't have to be away from their children all evening when their children are too young to be left at home. A second option is to use one home for the kids and a second home (close by or a phone call away) for the adults. A third idea is to rotate the responsibility of providing a lesson or care for the children either in the same home or in another home nearby. This can be an incredible blessing for kids. Finally, the most common idea is to decide that you need to have a night to invest in your spiritual life individually or as a couple and to make your own arrangements for child care. No matter what decision the group makes, the best approach is to dialogue openly about both the problem and the solution.

SMALL GROUP
AGREEMENT

Our Expectations:

To provide a predictable environment where participants experience authentic community and spiritual growth.

Group Attendance	To give priority to the group meeting. We will call or e-mail if we will be late or absent. (Completing the Small Group Calendar will minimize this issue.)
Safe Environment	To help create a safe place where people can be heard and feel loved. (Please, no quick answers, snap judgments, or simple fixes.)
Respect Differences	To be gentle and gracious to people with different spiritual maturity, personal opinions, temperaments, or "imperfections" in fellow group members. We are all works in progress.
Confidentiality	To keep anything that is shared strictly confidential and within the group, and to avoid sharing improper information about those outside the group.
Encouragement for Growth	To be not just takers but givers of life. We want to spiritually multiply our lives by serving others with our God-given gifts.
Shared Ownership	To remember that every member is a minister and to ensure that each attendee will share a small team role or responsibility over time.
Rotating Hosts/ Leaders and Homes	To encourage different people to host the group in their homes, and to rotate the responsibility of facilitating each meeting (see the Small Group Calendar).

Our Times Together:

- Refreshments _____
- Child care _____
- When we will meet (day of week) _____
- Where we will meet (place) _____
- We will begin at (time) _____ and end at _____
- We will do our best to have some or all of us attend a worship service together.

  Our primary worship service time will be _____
- Date of this agreement _____
- Date we will review this agreement again _____
- Who (other than the leader) will review this agreement at the end of this

  study _____

MEETING
STRUCTURE

Small groups gather not just to answer questions or to study a text, but to deepen their connection with God and with one another. We suggest that every meeting include not just study, but times of sharing, worship, and prayer. Every week, include the following elements:

SHARING

At your first or second meeting, use the Circles of Life diagram on the next page to write the names of two or three people you know who need to know Christ. Commit to pray for God's guidance and an opportunity to share with each of them. At subsequent meetings, check how group members are doing at reaching out to the people they've each listed on their circles chart.

PRAYER

Allow everyone to answer this question: "How can we pray for you this week?" Be sure to write prayer requests in each session's prayer segment.

WORSHIP

Spend a few minutes worshipping God together. Here are two ideas:

«   Have someone use their musical gifts to lead the group in a worship song. Try singing a cappella, using a worship CD, or have someone accompany your singing with a musical instrument.

«   Read a passage of Scripture together, making it a time of praise and worship as the words remind you of all God has done for you. Choose a psalm or other favorite verse.

CIRCLES OF
LIFE

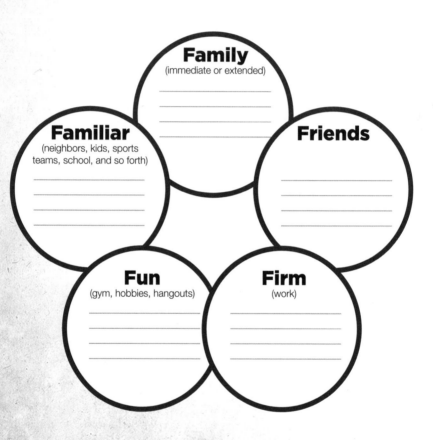

Family
(immediate or extended)

Familiar
(neighbors, kids, sports
teams, school, and so forth)

Friends

Fun
(gym, hobbies, hangouts)

Firm
(work)